Pumas

by Claire Archer

ABDO
BIG CATS
Kids

www.abdopublishing.com

Published by Abdo Kids, a division of ABDO, P.O. Box 398166, Minneapolis, Minnesota 55439.

Copyright © 2015 by Abdo Consulting Group, Inc. International copyrights reserved in all countries. No part of this book may be reproduced in any form without written permission from the publisher.

Printed in the United States of America, North Mankato, Minnesota.

052014

092014

 THIS BOOK CONTAINS RECYCLED MATERIALS

Photo Credits: Shutterstock, Thinkstock

Production Contributors: Teddy Borth, Jennie Forsberg, Grace Hansen

Design Contributors: Candice Keimig, Laura Rask, Dorothy Toth

Library of Congress Control Number: 2013952094

Cataloging-in-Publication Data

Archer, Claire.

 Pumas / Claire Archer.

  p. cm. -- (Big cats)

ISBN 978-1-62970-005-2 (lib. bdg.)

Includes bibliographical references and index.

1. Pumas--Juvenile literature.   I. Title.

599.75--dc23

2013952094

Table of Contents

Pumas

Pumas live in North and South America. Mountains are good places to find pumas.

5

Pumas are sometimes called mountain lions. They are also called cougars.

Pumas have thick fur. Their

fur keeps them warm.

Pumas can have light brown fur. Some pumas can be grayish or reddish. Their fur has no **markings**.

Big Cats

Pumas have large eyes.

Their ears are upright.

13

Pumas have large paws.

They have strong legs.

Pumas' back legs are longer than their front legs. This makes them good at jumping.

Hunting

Pumas **pounce** to catch their **prey**. They mainly eat small **mammals**.

19

Baby Pumas

Baby pumas are called **cubs**. Cubs are born with spots on their fur. Cubs leave their mothers at about two years old.

More Facts

- Pumas have more things in common with small cats than large cats. For example, pumas cannot roar. They hiss, growl, and whistle.

- **Cubs** are born with spots on their fur so their mothers can hide them in their habitats.

- Pumas can jump very high. They can jump about 20 feet (6 m) in the air!

Glossary

cub – a young animal.

mammal – a member of a group of living things. Mammals make milk to feed their babies and usually have hair or fur on their skin.

marking – a mark or pattern of marks on an animal's fur, feathers, or skin.

pounce – to spring or jump suddenly.

prey – an animal hunted or killed by a predator for food.

Index

abdokids.com

Use this code to log on to abdokids.com and access crafts, games, videos and more!

Abdo Kids Code:
BPK0052